READING

· FROM BRF ·

FOR THE
CHRISTMAS SEASON

Text copyright © BRF 2004

Published by
The Bible Reading Fellowship
First Floor, Elsfield Hall
15–17 Elsfield Way, Oxford OX2 8FG
ISBN 1 84101 357 9

First published 2004
10 9 8 7 6 5 4 3 2 1 0
All rights reserved

Acknowledgments
Scripture quotations taken from the *Holy Bible, New International Version*, copyright © 1973, 1978, 1984 by International Bible Society, are used by permission of Hodder & Stoughton Limited. All rights reserved. 'NIV' is a registered trademark of International Bible Society. UK trademark number 1448790.

Scripture quotations taken from The New Revised Standard Version of the Bible, Anglicized Edition, copyright © 1989, 1995 by the Division of Christian Education of the National Council of the Churches of Christ in the USA, are used by permission. All rights reserved.

Scripture quotations taken from The Revised Standard Version of the Bible, copyright © 1946; 1952, 1971 by the Division of Christian Education of the National Council of the Churches of Christ in the USA, are used by permission. All rights reserved.

Scripture quotations taken from the New Jerusalem Bible, published and copyright © 1985 by Darton, Longman and Todd Ltd and les Editions du Cerf, and by Doubleday, a division of Bantam Doubleday Dell Publishing Group, Inc. Used by permission of Darton, Longman and Todd Ltd, and Doubleday, a division of Random House, Inc.

A catalogue record for this book is available from the British Library

Printed and bound in Great Britain by
Bookmarque, Croydon

CONTENTS

GENERAL INTRODUCTION

Welcome to the new edition of BRF's Bible readings for the Christmas season.

At BRF we're passionate about helping you to put regular Bible reading and prayer at the heart of your spiritual journey.

The Bible is a wonderfully rich resource for inspiring prayer and worship, both individually and in fellowship with other members of the Christian Church, as well as being an invaluable guide for everyday life as we seek to grow closer to God.

So take a look at these sample readings from our three sets of Bible reading notes and our People's Bible Commentary series. With their fresh insights into familiar passages, we hope you'll find something here to encourage you to explore the Bible further in the weeks and months to come.

Lisa Cherrett

Lisa Cherrett
Managing Editor, Bible reading notes

Day by day
with God

DAILY BIBLE READING FOR WOMEN

Day by Day with God (published jointly with Christina Press) is written especially by women for women, with a regular team of contributors. Each four-monthly issue offers daily Bible readings, with key verses printed out, helpful comment and a prayer for the day ahead.

Our *Day by Day with God* extract contains readings for Christmas on the theme of 'Parties' (from the September–December 2004 notes), followed by a New Year's Day reading on 'Moulds' (slightly adapted from the January–April 2004 issue). The author, Chris Leonard, is married with two grown-up children. She has a degree in English and theology and her thirteen books range from biography and devotional to children's stories. She also enjoys leading creative writing workshops.

Parties

When she finds it, she calls her friends and neighbours together and says, 'Rejoice with me; I have found my lost coin.'

The great party season is upon us. How do you feel about that? Being a raving introvert at heart, the bigger and livelier the party, the more it saps my energy and makes me want to hibernate somewhere comfortable with a good book. Until way into the New Year, late night fireworks and shouting drunks from other people's parties will disturb my sleep. I hate the extra cooking and food shopping. I'll get fatter. I'll shout into ears of people I hardly know, then fix my face into an inane smile because I can't hear their replies in the hot, overcrowded room.

You can probably tell that I'm not exactly keen on parties. I'd much rather chat with a couple of good friends—though middle-aged partying does beat teenage days where everyone snogged, smoked and/or bopped in time to headache-making music.

Jesus loved parties. If he wasn't going to them, he was talking about them. All three of the 'lost' stories he told—sheep, coin and son—end with a party. It's the same with God in the Old Testament. All those Jerusalem feasts he set up—mega, nationwide parties with best barbequed meat at least thrice yearly. All the dancing he encouraged! The angels can certainly party, too—look what happened when Jesus was born and imagine being the bride at the wedding feast of the Lamb. There will be some parties in heaven!

Many festivities over the next couple of weeks will owe more to the debauched Roman festival of Saturnalia than to anything remotely Christian. However, Christmas is a time to rejoice and celebrate the fact that Jesus came to live on this earth for us and that people still worship him. They do that at Christmas more than at any other time of year.

....

Whether you're a party-lover or hate them, invite Jesus into your social life, including any parties you're going to this year.

CL

Self-pity

'Yet you never even gave me a young goat so I could celebrate with my friends.'

Today is my birthday. Unfortunately, it occurs on the same silly date every year. Although I'm not into parties, it would be nice to go out for a pub lunch with a couple of friends, but they're all like me—far too stressed, rushing round in circles, getting ready for Christmas. Anyway, all the local eateries are serving dried-up turkey to boozy office workers, accompanied by muzak dreams of a white Christmas that make me grind my teeth. The skies are grey, the ground muddy and people keep saying they're going down with the flu. Eeyore becomes my role model. No, Eeyore enjoyed being miserable and made his friends smile. Usually, in our house, some innocent bystander gets an earful.

Self-pity—it's so pathetic. I have so much to enjoy—including friends and family who love me. I could be full of thankfulness, but I'm like the whining older son in Jesus' story. He was always with his father. Everything his father had was his, yet he couldn't enter into the joy and celebration when his brother, who had lost all this, was found again.

My self-pitying gloom centres on a trivial issue, but Christmas is a truly difficult season for many people. Everyone is 'supposed' to be having a wonderful time, but for those who have suffered loss, all the parties and fun can rub salt in raw wounds. I guess, though, anyone who, with God's help, resists resentment at others' joy and then finds something to celebrate—Jesus' birth, for example—will be walking in God's ways and may even feel better, too!

Lord, you have pity on us always, so there's no need for us to wallow in miserable self-pity, even if there is a good reason. Help those who, for whatever reason, struggle with parties and celebrations this year. Encourage each of us with glimpses of the Father's joy and celebration as we celebrate his son's birthday.

Best wine for the party

Nearby stood six stone water jars, the kind used by the Jews for ceremonial washing, each holding from twenty to thirty gallons.

You know how toddlers love being whooshed through the air and tipped upside down? I find that, surprisingly often, reading the Bible has a similar effect. Well, Jesus did say we have to be like little children to enter his kingdom...

At a village wedding, Jesus makes about 150 gallons of vintage Château Bar-Joseph. How many people would have been at the party—surely not more than 300? That's half a gallon, or over two litres, each—and they'd already drunk the original intoxicants dry. How outrageous, tipping my 'correct Christian morality' upside down! Both Old and New Testaments contain plenty of evidence that God hates drunkenness. What was Jesus doing?

John says that Jesus was doing the first of his miraculous signs, revealing his glory so that the disciples put their faith in him. Cynics might say, 'Young men would follow a guy who performed this kind of party trick!' but more is going on here. Jesus turned 150 gallons of water for Jewish ceremonial washing (imagine carting that from the well!) into the intoxicating wine of the gospel. It reminds me of Peter having to explain on the Jewish feast of Pentecost, 'These men are not drunk, as you suppose. It's only nine in the morning!' (Acts 2:15).

This 'sign' shows us a lot about Jesus—and his Father. Not the kind of God who spoils the party by telling the kids to wash their hands all the time, instead he enhances celebrations, transforming them from black and white to Technicolor. His generosity runs to extravagance—especially towards people who are poor and oppressed—and he is surprising. We're not following a set of rules, we're following a wonderful God-man. He whooshes his children to the moon and back quite safely while they chuckle and ask for more.

....

Read Ephesians 5:18. Ask God to help you stay child-like this Christmas—and drunk, on the Holy Spirit, of course!

CL

Costly party

The Son of Man came eating and drinking, and you say, 'Here is a glutton and a drunkard, a friend of tax collectors and "sinners".'

A water-into-wine party piece could sound cheap—and someone has to pay the price for the kind of superabundant grace we were thinking about yesterday. John the Baptist was in prison when he sent to ask his cousin, Jesus, 'Are you the one who is to come or should we expect someone else?' John's mission, understood almost from the womb, was to prepare the way for the Messiah by urging people to repent and be baptized. Not a party-lover but an ascetic prophet, first living in the desert, then imprisoned for doing God's work, John paid a huge price—his life, finally. However, it wasn't enough. Jesus said that none born of women was greater than John, 'yet the one who is least in the kingdom of God is greater than he'. He also remarked that John 'came neither eating bread nor drinking wine, and you say, "He has a demon."'

Cousin Jesus, by contrast, was accused of partying, eating and drinking too much, mixing with sinful people who lived it up. He reached many, but that wasn't quite enough either.

Today, we kingdom people who are 'greater than John the Baptist' (!) regularly drink wine together. It signifies the blood of one who loved to mix with sinners but was himself entirely free from sin. As we swallow that wine, it's as though we are allowing the pure life of Jesus to flow within us. He lived life to the full. Our intoxication with the Holy Spirit is only possible because of his amazing sacrifice. His miracle grace is anything but cheap.

He calls us to take up our cross and follow him. Following him means partying with and befriending sinners, which may well be harder spiritually than joining a desert nunnery.

....

Jesus, thank you for mixing with and then dying for us sinners, that we might enjoy knowing you and experience your holy life—life in all its fullness.

CL

Party behaviour

He was being carefully watched...

People-watching at parties can be fun. Some very religious people watched Jesus at a party meal. Hardly the politest of guests, he waded straight in, challenging deeply held beliefs with direct questions and action. Talk about causing social embarrassment! I imagine that the guest who was healed of dropsy (where watery fluid collects in the body's cavities or tissues) enjoyed the best party ever—after he was 'sent away'. Sadly, the prominent Pharisee host couldn't rejoice with him. The atmosphere at his party must have become decidedly strained, especially as Jesus, having done some people-watching of his own, offered unasked-for advice that overturned what were deemed to be the correct standards of Pharisaic etiquette, pouring shame on host and guests alike.

Pharisees strove to obey the rules of God and man, doing everything decently and in order. At a party meal, they would make sure that they gave people the correct places of honour. Jesus upset the carefully worked-out seating plan by advising everyone to take the lowest place. Imagine the chaos that would cause! Then he informed his host that he'd invited the wrong kind of people anyway. If he wanted God's reward, why ask respectable folk who would invite him back? He should have filled the place with outcasts—the poor, crippled, lame and blind—those less than perfect who were normally pushed to, or over, the edge of Jewish religious and social life.

This story raises the uncomfortable question, what kind of people do we invite to meals or parties? I know we see the word 'Pharisee' and read 'baddie', but I feel some sympathy here and wonder, had I been hostess that day, might I have begun to consider Jesus to be the guest to dread?

Thank you, Jesus, that you love all people so much. I want to follow your heart, rather than social, cultural or religious rules. Where I'm blind, show me. In particular, show me exactly who to include in the warmth of your love over this Christmas season.

CL

Party invitations

Go out into the roads and country lanes and make them come in.

I wonder in what tone of voice his fellow guest responded to Jesus' words that those who invite outcasts to their banquet will be blessed and repaid at the resurrection of the righteous? 'Blessed is the man who will eat at the feast in the kingdom of God.' Was his tone longing (if only I could be there) or sanctimonious (as a son of Abraham, I'm home and dry, mate)?

Whichever one it was, he did not understand that Jesus had made God's kingdom present as well as future. The Father gave the world the biggest gift, the biggest party ever, in sending Jesus. However, many who claimed to be God's chosen ones weren't accepting the gift or the invitation. Their excuses varied from 'I'm too busy or important' to 'It's wrong to heal on the Sabbath'. So, in telling the parable of the great banquet, I wonder if Jesus' tone was angry.

I'm not sure God ever does make anyone come to his party. However, people do need someone to go proactively, to explain who exactly has invited them—and impact them with the truth that they are more than welcome. It hurts us, too, when, as 'beggars showing other beggars where to find bread' at his table, rich or poor ones turn away, but we never know. 'Did I once sit next to you at a Chamber of Commerce dinner, Chris?' a shop owner asked me when he learnt which road and church I used to inhabit. I'd never been to such a dinner; it must have been my former next-door neighbour, Carrie, over 15 years ago. 'I've been a Christian just three years—but it all began with that conversation,' he explained. When I phoned Carrie she said, 'Oh Chris, I never feel I do anything much!'

We'll meet many people in the next few days, Lord—friends, harassed sales staff, family members who annoy or appal us. Enable us to be your invitation bearers.

CL

Christmas praise party

**Sing to the Lord a new song, his praise
in the assembly of the saints.**

The Old Testament praise party described in this psalm sounds exuberant—singing, dancing, tambourine, harp... Under the new covenant, we can celebrate even more! On Christmas day, we open the presents, but it's Jesus' birthday party. When our children were little, we used to sing 'Happy birthday to Jesus' as a family. It's an old, familiar song—as so many of our Christmas carols are. ('Carol' means 'dance'.) I guess God doesn't become as tired of hearing carols and other praise songs as I imagine British royalty must do of musical pleas to 'Save the Queen'. Whatever the case, why not let your hair down and celebrate by singing Jesus a new song today, by yourself on your bed or with other partying Christians in joyful assembly?

All this happy-clappy praise partying—isn't it about as enduring and useful as the bubbles in a glass of Christmas champagne? These days my grown-up son demands to know what kind of a god wants people praising him morning, noon and night. They are fair questions —and maybe this psalm contains part of an answer. Maybe heartfelt praise is a weapon of our spiritual warfare. That's easy to see on a personal level because it's hard to really praise God while maintaining a blinkered, selfish perspective or other bad attitude. As we praise him, our hope and faith rises. Despite the sad or terrible things that we may see around, we are declaring that we know he is Lord, he is good, he loves, he acts, he crowns the humble with salvation, he even takes delight in us! Remember that, whether you're rushing about feeding what feels like 5000 or struggling with loneliness, alone or in a crowd.

....

Read the new song that poured from Mary's mouth when she shared with her cousin the amazing news that she was bearing God's child (Luke 1:46–55). Enter into her joy and let your own spill out—for he still does lift up the humble and fills the hungry with good things.

CL

ESTHER 5:1–8; 7:1–10 (NIV)

Party politics

So the king and Haman went to dine with Queen Esther, and as they were drinking wine on that second day the king again asked, 'Queen Esther, what is your petition?'

Not all parties in the Bible are given for lame ducks. Here, Esther is entertaining despotic King Xerxes and his scheming henchman, Haman. True, the king is her husband, but she's no longer his favourite wife and one word from him could spell her death. She's also Jewish—her ancestors were carried into exile and her people are now subjects of Xerxes' vast kingdom, which comprises '127 provinces stretching from India to Cush' (1:1). Haman's machinations mean that her people are under a death sentence. Feeling totally inadequate, Esther finds that she is the only person who might save them. Her uncle asks, 'Who knows but that you have come to royal position for such a time as this?' A brave woman, Esther uses the weapons at her disposal—her best dress and two fine banquets—to play 'party' politics, save her people and ensure that Haman meets the fate he deserves.

I hope that your entertaining over the festive season will be in less dramatic circumstances, but it could still be strategic in terms of God's purposes. If you have guests and are feeling that you might as well be a potato-peeling machine or chambermaid, remember that some have entertained angels unawares. Think of Mary and Martha who provided a home from home for Jesus and his friends, or the two women who did the same for Elisha (2 Kings 4). Those who gave hospitality to the 72 disciples Jesus sent out in pairs were healed and welcomed into God's kingdom. If you're a guest, perhaps travelling a distance with fretful children, pray that peace will be on the house where you're staying.

....

Being hospitable demands skill, tact and hard work. Being a guest isn't always easy, but God cares about both! Invite him to use the hospitality you're offering—and/or your experience of being a guest—during this festive season.

CL

Immoral parties

Woe to those who are heroes at drinking wine and champions at mixing drinks, who acquit the guilty for a bribe, but deny justice to the innocent.

Wine is good—here God is seen as vineyard tender and winemaker and we know that he loves parties. Good gifts can be twisted and abused, though. They certainly were in the eighth century BC when Isaiah was writing. People called good evil and evil good: 'Getting drunk is great—who cares about justice, truth or the poor?' Isaiah's words sound distressingly familiar in the 21st century AD where a good night out for many is a binge-drinking session, following which the 'weak' need their stomachs pumped and the 'strong' get into fights. Those who don't join in the more extreme clubbing/party scene are seen as weirdo killjoys or, at best, ignorant.

'Don't knock it till you've tried it!' I've been told by young adults. Well, I'm sorry, I wouldn't enjoy the vomiting, hangovers, crude, aggressive side of personalities coming to the fore, and damage, either creeping or sudden. This isn't light, it's darkness. It isn't sweet, but bitter. It was bad enough when I was a teenager, but what with drugs and 'ladettes' outdoing 'laddish culture', it's worse now. Please pray for 'Generation X'.

God said, 'Woe to those who rise early in the morning to run after their drinks, who stay up late at night till they are inflamed by wine.' Massive woe does come to alcoholics and to those who love them. 'They have harps and lyres at their banquets, tambourines and flute and wine' (or electric guitars, sound systems and drugs) 'but they have no regard for the deeds of the Lord, no respect for the work of his hands.' No respect for the people he made or even for their own bodies. If we're not in awe of our creator God, unhealthy, evil things can so easily fill the gap.

....

Pray for the empty ones this party season. Pray especially for those who habitually abuse alcohol and/or drugs—and for those who love them.

CL

Parties when you're hurting

**Why do the wicked... make merry to the sound of the flute...
spend their years in prosperity and go down
to the grave in peace.**

This is such a difficult time of year for many people. Friends may be away with their families. The normal routine usually stops for a week or so while everyone is supposedly enjoying themselves. There must be plenty who want to throw something at the jolly togetherness splurging from their TV screens—those who are bereaved or divorced, singles stuck caring for infirm parents, those who are ill or in some kind of institution, even those in a foreign country far from home.

We've read Isaiah where he's railing against immoral parties, but the people Job describes don't sound especially wicked: 'Their homes are safe and free from fear... their little ones dance about.' Their parties appear fine—not at all like drunken orgies—but Job has lost all his family, health and possessions. When he sees other people enjoying themselves, it rankles. Surely, it's unfair—these people don't want to know God and yet all is well with them, whereas Job tried his best to know and serve God and look what happened!

Yes, life is unfair; some of the best people suffer the most terrible calamities. We can spend forever trying to work out why, but we do know that, whatever individuals are going through, God longs to be with them—comforting those who mourn, weeping with those who weep, befriending the lonely, strengthening the weak. He needs us sometimes—to be his arms giving people a hug, doing their shopping or sitting with them in silence, during this Christmas season and also through the months to come.

....

Lord, we pray for all who for various sad reasons aren't going to enjoy the festivities this year. Help us to be sensitive and remember those we can draw alongside with tenderness, as you yourself do. Help us to comfort others with the comfort you have given us.

CL

Good reason to party!

Then he went with them into the temple courts, walking and jumping, and praising God.

Some terrible scenes had happened in the temple courts not long before. A furious Jesus saw callous traders exploiting poor worshippers and violently cleansed what should have been sacred space. Then he was tried in the court of the high priest while, outside, Peter disowned him three times.

Jesus, who brought healing and new life to so many; Jesus whom many believed to be the Messiah who would rescue them from the hated Roman occupiers, was condemned to death, then crucified. Now a beggar, aged over 40, who isn't allowed into the temple because he's been disabled from birth, is healed instantly in Jesus' name by Peter of all people! No wonder the former beggar is having his own personal praise party, leaping and shouting all over the temple. He's never had anything to celebrate before. No wonder, too, that people are running to see him—and staying to hear more about this Jesus who still saves and heals people even though he died. They don't understand yet that Jesus rose from the grave and ascended into heaven, but they do understand that this man who has sat begging at the Beautiful Gate for so many years is bouncing around like a six-year-old.

Who knows why sometimes God is with us, drawing alongside, bringing comfort but not removing our distress and why, at other times, he works a miracle and turns someone's mourning or sickness literally into dancing? All we know here is that, after this miracle, 'the number of men' (who believed) 'grew to about 5000' (4:4). Before that, 3000 had been saved at Pentecost and others were 'added daily', but this particular miracle caused enough of a stir to worry the religious authorities deeply.

....

Let's pray for miracles that will draw people's attention to the fact that Jesus lives and cares and loves people today. And when they happen, let's really party!

CL

ACTS 2:43–47 (NIV)

Ongoing party

Every day they continued to meet together in the temple courts. They broke bread in their homes and ate together with glad and sincere hearts, praising God and enjoying the favour of all the people.

OK, we've just gone backwards in Acts, but it seems to me that the baby Church, which formed after the 3000 were saved at Pentecost, enjoyed an ongoing party. It may have been quieter than the beggar who jumped and praised God, but it was the best kind of party. The new Christians were 'together'. They had 'everything in common'. Some parties are designed to show off wealth, but in this one they sold what they had and gave to anyone in need.

I saw a couple on breakfast television today. Having won £7.6 million at Lotto, they spent some on themselves, but gave a considerable amount to family and charities. 'What's the point having money festering in a bank when it could be doing good?' the couple said. 'Giving it away and seeing the good it does makes us really happy.' The TV presenters seemed amazed, but delighted with them. 'What lovely people!' they said.

Parties don't have to be elaborate. Meeting together is all you need for a great party. Sharing bread in each other's homes is more than enough. Caring for each other and anyone in need, concentrating on giving not getting, will make any party special. Praising God together with glad and sincere hearts guarantees a great party. The new Christians had reason to be glad—not only was Jesus alive but also miracles were being done by apostles who, until a few days before, had been hiding away, useless, frightened. The Holy Spirit transformed them into bold ambassadors for Jesus. He gave them, not the Dutch courage of alcohol, but something far more amazing that meant Peter had to explain, 'These men are not drunk as you suppose. It's only nine in the morning!' (Acts 2:15).

....

Thank you, Lord, that, while there are people following you, there's no reason for your amazing party to stop!

CL

Wedding party

**'Blessed are those who are invited to the
wedding supper of the Lamb!'**

Will you be seeing the New Year in, either at home or at a party?
Personally I fail to see what is so exciting about one number turning
into another number. I'd rather not sing the unintelligible words of
Auld Lang Syne, dodging the debris of party poppers while my feet
are trampled by tipsy strangers. I prefer to fall asleep well before
midnight if fireworks and revellers allow. A wedding, though, now
that is something to dress up for, celebrate, cheer about, weep tears
of joy over—especially a wedding where you are the bride!

After all, what's a New Year, when time itself will be made new?
There will be new heavens, a new earth and a new dress for the
bride, of 'fine linen, bright and clear'. Forget New Year resolutions,
you'll be given clothes of righteousness. Forget careful make-up and
hairdos or the fact that you're feeling a year older—you'll become
'radiant', 'without stain or wrinkle or any other blemish' (Ephesians
5:27). Forget yourself and remember who it is that you are going to
marry! For you are part of the Church universal, who is Christ's
beloved bride. It's way beyond the capacity of our thoughts or
imagination, this wedding supper of the Lamb, but we know that it's
been devised by our Father—our creator God—who loves us and his
son. Not a quiet affair, the noise that the multitude of heavenly and
earthly beings make will sound 'like the roar of rushing waters and
like loud peals of thunder'. It takes place in the heaven they made
together for us all to enjoy and you and I are invited. It's going to be
some party!

Enjoy your party or your quiet night in but, if you keep on living
with this wedding party in your heart, it will transform your life!

....

*Father, thank you for making a place just for me at your son's
wedding feast. Let that hope surge through my life like champagne
bubbles throughout the coming year.*

CL

What shape is your mould?

For I resolved to know nothing while I was with you except Jesus Christ and him crucified. I came to you in weakness and fear, and with much trembling.

New Year resolutions—stick to that diet and exercise plan, give up smoking plus whatever caused the current hangover, go easier on the credit cards, be true to yourself and nice to everyone. Those who keep such resolutions should fit into a slim, healthy, acceptable mould. With luck and really hard work some could be smiling fit to grace glossy women's magazines. Christians may well be resolving to pray more, to get up early every single morning to study the Bible and to be very, very good. Whether Christian or not, I suspect most resolution-makers will end up feeling, not better, but guilty and discouraged.

Paul's resolve was based, not on his own strength of determination but on a man crucified shamefully as a common criminal. That's just not the thing to aim for, is it? Our culture screams that death, weakness, fear and trembling are to be avoided. Surely we need to become strong, intelligent and acceptable, in order to spread the good news about Jesus with wise and persuasive words? Well, actually, no, implies Paul in the next verse. He relied on 'a demonstration of the Spirit's power, so that your faith might not rest on men's wisdom, but on God's power'.

Stop and think for a moment about 'moulds'—about the pressure to conform in one way or another. What 'moulds' are people trying to squeeze themselves into in these early years of the 21st century? What are 'acceptable' Christian moulds? And if, as Paul suggests, the only 'mould' which is also acceptable to God is the extraordinary figure of Jesus himself, what does that mean to us, practically?

....

Jesus, thank you that I don't have to squeeze myself by my own efforts into being something I'm not—you'd rather have someone who, knowing she's weak and inadequate, trusts in your saving grace.

CL

Guidelines

Guidelines is a unique Bible reading resource that offers four months of in-depth study written by leading scholars. Contributors are drawn from around the world as well as the UK, and represent a stimulating and thought-provoking breadth of Christian tradition. Instead of dated daily readings, *Guidelines* provides weekly units, broken into at least six sections, plus an introduction giving context for the passage, and a final section of points for thought and prayer. On any day you can read as many or as few sections as you wish. As well as a copy of *Guidelines*, you will need a Bible, as the passage is not included.

The *Guidelines* extracts in this sampler are taken from the September–December 2004 issue, in which Anne Roberts writes on the theme of Advent, and Christopher Hancock on Christmas. Anne Roberts is a freelance writer and teacher in further and higher education. For many years she had responsibility for teaching and training in an Anglican church in Bolton. Christopher Hancock is Dean of Bradford Cathedral. He has a particular commitment to education in multi-faith and international contexts.

ADVENT

We may often have begun Advent resolved to take more time to meditate on those familiar stories concerning the most amazing event ever to have occurred on our planet—the coming into our world of God himself, incarnate as a human baby—but events take over and we come to Boxing Day, having missed the opportunity once more. We feel we'd have been more true to the spirit of the season if we had taken time to prepare in a more fitting fashion. It may be that this will be the year when we arrive at Christmas Day with a sense of wonder, induced by delving in a deeper way into what Luke and Matthew so meticulously recorded for us and seeing how this was all in fulfilment of God's promises to his people. Perhaps we will give God the attention he deserves, considering the awesome nature of what these stories tell us he did.

Quotations are from the NIV Bible.

13–19 DECEMBER

1 Joy shared

Luke 1:57–66

The village is buzzing! They have pitied Elizabeth in the past. Perhaps there has been embarrassment as their children have played in front of her house and they've seen her anguish as she's watched. Now they can all rejoice with her. A baby—and a son at that! God's merciful kindness has been poured out on her. And they don't yet know the half of it. The villagers gather for the party at which the child will be named and circumcised. It's a great day for everyone.

The day turns out to be a day of surprises as well as joy. The assumption is that the child will be named after his father Zechariah. The family and neighbours are astonished when Elizabeth gives a name which seems to have been picked out of the blue. Only when Zechariah confirms that the boy's name is to be John do they accept it.

The astonishment grows as Zechariah's tongue is loosed. Evidence is accumulating that a great act of God is under way.

Zechariah has emerged from the holy place deaf and mute; the ageing Elizabeth has a son; the child's totally unexpected name means 'God has shown favour' and the father's tongue is loosed. The tale spreads like a bush fire and people all around are on edge, wondering what is about to happen in and through this child.

There is a strong sense of community in this story. Faith and village life are interwoven. The people know themselves to be God's people, and joy and sadness are shared. A circumcision was a day of supreme importance in all of this, since by it the child became a member of God's covenant community and the parents placed him under the law that undergirded the community. It was commitment to God, to his law and to each other that made the village a community.

We can learn from this. Today's society is disjointed. Many in our world are without community, and no one is committed to them. Some prefer it that way, but Christmas is a time when we can make extra efforts to include those who don't.

2 He has come

Luke 1:67–75

'He has come… has redeemed… has raised up a horn of salvation.' I think we must assume that Gabriel's words to Mary, Elizabeth's greeting of Mary and Mary's own 'Magnificat' were known to Zechariah, despite his deafness. All three will have been wondering whether God's day of salvation has arrived. The Holy Spirit fills Zechariah; he knows the day has come, and declares it. In the child Mary carries is the long-awaited redemption of God's people.

Zechariah declares them saved from the enemies who have trapped and controlled them. As God's covenant family they have been promised victory over their enemies and that they will be a blessing to all nations (Deuteronomy 7:16–18). In being saved, they will be free to worship and serve God and to live holy and righteous lives, according to his law. There would be no fear of being prevented from doing so by their former enemies.

Zechariah may have imagined freedom from Rome and the setting up of a Jewish state. Perhaps he had already learnt that God does not always, or even often, do things in the way we imagine. He may have had a realistic notion that his own child and Mary's would be rejected like most of the prophets before them. He may have realized that, like most prophecies, his own would be partly realized in the immediate future, partly in the distant future, in ways he cannot yet envisage and only fully in the new age. However, he was most certainly filled with faith, able to praise God and to trust him to fulfil his promises in his way and time.

We still live in the 'now but not yet' of God's salvation plan. We know that God has come and has saved us in and through his Son. We enjoy many benefits of this salvation. But there are no guarantees yet that we shall not suffer at the hands of our enemies or that it will be easy to live holy and righteous lives. Advent reminds us that Christ has come but is still to come. Only at that second coming shall we see the final consummation of God's plan to prepare 'his people, his treasured possession' (1 Peter 2:4–9; Deuteronomy 7:6).

3 A prepared way

Luke 1:76–79

Zechariah now tells something of how God's salvation is to come to them. Many doting parents, looking at their child, feel their hearts swell at what they believe the child will become. Zechariah's conviction is from the Holy Spirit and certain of fulfilment. Jesus will be 'the Son of the Most High' (Luke 1:32). His own son John will be 'the prophet of the Most High', declaring that the Lord is on the way. Just as the arrival of a great dignitary demands physical preparations, the arrival of the Lord requires preparation of the heart. God has played his part throughout Israel's history and now does so in John, who is to bring about the final stage in the preparations. He will declare that the forgiveness of sins is to be made possible by God's tender mercy.

The picture is of people living in the darkness of night. They are kept from living in the light of God's love by oppression and sin. Death casts a 24-hour shadow, with no certainty of what lies beyond it. Now the sun will rise and no one will need to live in the shadows again. 'The people walking in darkness have seen a great light; on those living in the land of the shadow of death a light has dawned' (Isaiah 9:2). Zechariah sees the fulfilment of that messianic prophecy in the child to be born to Mary. The light will guide God's people along the path of peace, and so they will be able to live in that holiness and righteousness spoken of earlier.

Assumed in Zechariah's prophecy is a conviction of sin. The people are aware that sin separates them from God. They want to lead holy and righteous lives, but are hampered in doing so by this inclination to sin. God comes down not in judgment but in tender mercy. He wants them to be assured that sins can be forgiven and the way has been made open for them to walk with him in peace. In the spirit of Advent we can ask ourselves if God wants us to become aware of our need for the forgiveness of particular sins, so that he can come in a new way into our hearts.

4 Sunrise

Malachi 4:1–6

The hope expressed by Zechariah, Elizabeth and Mary would have derived partly from Malachi's prophecy concerning God's way of fulfilling his promises to his people. The prophecy addresses the people's complaints at God's perceived failure to fulfil his word to them, and goes on to show how he will one day do so.

Babylon lies in the past. The temple has been rebuilt. But where is the blessing? Why are we just a nowhere backwater of a mighty empire? They question God's love (Malachi 1:2). They show contempt for his name (1:6). Their worship is sacrilegious (1:7). They are fed up with bringing sacrifices and when they do they bring sickly animals (1:12–14). The priests are false teachers (2:1–9). The people have intermarried with those who worship other gods and are unfaithful to marriage. They then moan because God doesn't seem to pay them any attention any more (2:11–16). To these sins they add oppression of the under-privileged and meanness in refusing to bring their tithes to God (3:5–9). They are totally unrepentant. Which came first? Did they begin to neglect God only when he didn't come up with the goods? So they say.

God suggests they test him by bringing in their tithes and seeing if the situation will not change (3:10–12). If they respond to this, as God's treasured possession they will see justice prevail (3:16–18).

Coming to today's reading, God says that the day will come when, in the fires of judgment, the stubble will burn up—but those who revere his name will bask in the light of the sun of righteousness. The healing of their sadness and desolation will be in his wings. Spiritual youth will be renewed. From dragging themselves around in the darkness, they will leap around like young animals unleashed or released from the stall.

In the time of John and Jesus, the people still had the same complaints against God, to which they would add 400 years of heavenly silence. The Gospels show that the temple was still abused and folk made excuses for not tithing. There was little social justice. But there were those who were faithfully waiting for the sun to rise, and Zechariah announced his arrival. Jesus would say that John was the Elijah who was to come. Is this the great and dreadful day of the Lord? Malachi warns that if the people do not repent in the light of the sun's rising, the land itself will be cursed. Did the society of Jesus' day take note? Should our society be taking note?

5 Root and branch

Isaiah 11:1–10

Isaiah has spoken at length of the threat from Assyria. He assures God's people that even if the Davidic dynasty falls to the Assyrians, this will not be the end of the story.

A leader will arrive on the scene who will have a sevenfold (perfect) endowment of the Spirit. He will have wisdom, with the understanding to see into the heart of any matter (v. 2a). He will have the ability to see what needs to be done and the wherewithal to do it (v. 2b). He will have a deep sense of who is who and what is what in spiritual and moral terms, leading to reverence and obedience (v. 2c). His crowning glory and the seventh aspect of his filling will be that his whole delight will be in the fear of the Lord (v. 3). In this fear he lives out the gifts of the Spirit, showing wisdom to discern between appearance and reality, understanding of what lies behind what is said, counsel in what is fair for the downtrodden, power of command in executing the appropriate justice and a deep underlying knowledge of how things are in the world.

The belt, or sash (v. 5), represents readiness for action. Loose, flowing garments needed to be girded up if there was a need to hurry or to get down to work. This promised leader is always ready to act on behalf of righteousness and faithfulness.

Old enmities cease. Wolf and lamb, leopard and goat offer hospitality to one another. It doesn't take a farmer or zookeeper to handle them, but a child can lead them. Cows and bears, lions and oxen eat together—and this is no uneasy truce between adults. They will bring their children (yearlings) with them and pass on the new understanding to the next generation. The defenceless infant and the daring toddler will be left by parents to play in what were once the most dangerous places. The enmity between the seed of the woman and the seed of the serpent (Genesis 3:15) is no more. Eden is restored!

Who is the one who brings in this new world? He comes from the same source as David—the stump or root of Jesse. But he is more—he is the Root of Jesse himself (v. 10). He was before Jesse, the very origin of David's line. Is it any wonder that when this Root arrives, all harmful and destructive influences and actions will cease? Instead of them, the earth will be filled with that knowledge of the Lord that leads to the fear of the Lord in which will be all our delight. Mary had a taste of that delight (Luke 1:47). We can taste it too, because the Root has come—and will come!

6 God with us!

Matthew 1:18–25

There was no doubt in Joseph's mind! Sorrow and disappointment were in his heart, certainly, but no doubt in his mind. Mary (and her unborn child) had to go. The betrothal contract was binding; he was already her husband (v. 19). Joseph's conclusion, being told of Mary's condition, was that she had committed adultery. The procedure laid down by Moses was to have her publicly judged and stoned. In light of this, Joseph's proposed action—to divorce her quietly—was the only charitable way forward.

How many such cases were dealt with in the harsher way, we do not know. Joseph had the right to demand it. Some would expect it of him. His heart of love and grace would not allow it. Joseph's choice indicated that the love and grace of the forgiving God were already in him. However churned up and grieving, he did not stand on his rights and use the law to vindicate himself. He 'let go'—the ultimate meaning of the act of forgiveness. He let go of the apparent injury (even insult) to himself and handed it to God for him to deal with. We have far more evidence that Joseph had of God's willingness to forgive us. We have no excuse not to do as he did when we are mistreated or disappointed.

As we approach Christmas, Matthew presents us with a God

who speaks. He has reminded us that God speaks in history (1:1–17). How much of God comes to mind when we look at those names and recall their stories—stories of sin and redemption, of failure and recovery—through which God revealed himself. We see here too a God who speaks in dreams (v. 20). Far from the first instance in scripture, it will not be the last either. God speaks through angels; God speaks through scripture (vv. 20, 22). None of this was new to Matthew's readers. But this time God speaks through a Son.

What God speaks through his Son is declared upfront in the Son's name—salvation from sin. In and through the speaking he has done since the day of creation, God has always been proactive. His speech is creative and redemptive, because it carries his authority. This time, though, he goes further. He doesn't only speak to us, he becomes one of us—Immanuel. It can be said that, in a greater way than ever before, God is as good as his word. He now intends to display, in a new and unmistakable way, that he means what he says.

Guidelines

The child leapt in my womb.
He did!
I know I haven't been pregnant before
but I do know that unborn babies
jump around at times.
This was not that.
Believe me, I knew!
I couldn't help but shout!
    'Mary!
Blessed you are among women
and blessed the child you bear!
You come to me as mother of my lord!
I know it.
My child knows it.
The joy we feel is heaven's joy.
As virgin you will bear a child
and blessed are you that you believe!'
And blessed are you, Holy Spirit,
that you reveal these things to me.
I share my neighbours' awe.

What will these children be?
What will be their joy?
What will be their sorrow
and what their end?
I only know that God intends to walk on earth
and one prepares the way for him to come.
Can it be…?

Turn our hearts, O Lord; turn our hearts and make them ready that
your coming day may bring us life and not death.

Zechariah, Elizabeth, Mary, Joseph—they stand at the turning-point of history. They are prepared in heart and mind through their knowledge of God's word, belief in his promises and the obedience of faith, no matter what the cost. It is likely that Zechariah, Elizabeth and Joseph did not live to see the way their sons' lives ended. Mary did. But she also witnessed her own son's resurrection. She would be the one to see the proof, in signs and wonders, in radical teachings, in death and in resurrection, that her son was indeed 'God with us'. We too have seen—and will see!

CHRISTMAS

Here, we look at Christmas through the first chapter of John's Gospel, which gives a different perspective from the normal 'Christmas story' readings in Luke and Matthew. In this week's readings, running up to Christmas Day itself, we will examine John's 'prologue'—the first eighteen verses, in which he sets out who Jesus is and the purpose of his birth.

Quotations are taken from the NIV Bible.

20–26 DECEMBER

1 Letting God be God

John 1:1–5

Among the most famous words we hear at Christmas are those that begin our study of John 1: 'In the beginning was the Word, and the Word was with God, and the Word was God.' Genesis 1 echoes loud and clear. John 1:1–5 is like a fanfare at the start of a pageant. We're meant to sit up and listen. Something important is about to happen. We are in the presence of royalty. With solemn beauty John introduces Jesus Christ, the Word, as co-eternal with God (v. 2) and co-creator of all (v. 3).

John's description of Jesus Christ as 'Word of God' is pivotal. At the start of his evangelistic Gospel (20:30–31), John deliberately presents Jesus as the 'Word of God' to connect both with Jewish theology (in which God's 'Word' was the dynamic speech and act of God in history) and with Greek philosophy (where the concept of 'the Word' was at the heart of the rationality and coherence of the world). It's stunning stuff, enriched by John's claim that in Jesus God's 'light' (v. 5) and 'life' (v. 4) are found. As scholars point out, the first paragraph (vv. 1–5) of John's Prologue (1:1–18) is thoroughly theological: it's all about God. The canvas is vast; the intention is clear: set no boundaries to your thinking about what follows. We are dealing with God. In Jesus, God and history meet. In him, time and eternity intersect.

What a wonderful place from which to prepare for Christmas! For the great mystery and miracle of Christmas begin not in a stall at Bethlehem, or a pew in a church, but in the life, love and purpose of God. 'Begin Christmas at the beginning,' John would say to us. 'Begin with God.' It's like the corner-piece of the Christmas jigsaw—this is the place to start. It's like pitching the right note before you sing carols. How sad when Christmas gets off to a terrible start because it doesn't begin with God.

2 The messenger

John 1:6–8

A dramatic shift occurs between the first and second paragraphs of John's Prologue. Verses 1–5 are about 'the Word' and work of God; verses 6–8 focus on the life and ministry of a man. 'There came a man who was sent from God; his name was John.' As if in a great play, John the Baptist steps out of the mystery of God's will on to the stage of history. His importance cannot be exaggerated, as his position here in John's Prologue suggests. Indeed, he figures prominently throughout John 1 (see vv. 19–34).

It was important that John's Gospel should clarify the Baptist's role, for he attracted followers long after his death and left some Christians confused. Crucially, he is presented here as God's appointed 'witness' (vv. 7–8). The word 'witness' is the meaning of the Greek 'martyr'—an apt description for a man who staked all on the truthfulness of his testimony to Jesus as God's 'true light' for the world. But, as John makes unequivocally clear, he was not the light; rather 'he came only as a witness to the light' (v. 8). The Baptist is like the best kind of biographer, the self-effacing witness to the life and work of another.

If John's Prologue calls Christians first (as Martin Luther put it) to 'Let God be God!', verses 6–8 call for humble recognition of the role God graciously accords humans in his work. 'There came a man... his name was John'. It could be Philip or Diana, Bill or Wendy. God shares his work with faithful individuals. He could manage without us, but he chooses to involve us. In John the Baptist we see a living and dying example of the faithful witness who 'endured to the end'. In honouring him we should honour and remember all who have followed in his martyr's steps. We may not be called to suffer physically; we are called to witness faithfully. We may not have the leading role of a Jesus or a John; we still have a part in God's great drama of salvation. We may wonder how worthy is our 'witness', but we still have that role to play.

3 The true light

John 1:9–11

From John the Baptist the Prologue moves to Jesus, 'the true light that gives light to everyone' (v. 9). Light is a wonderful image for Jesus and prominent in John's Gospel. As Jesus proclaims, 'I am the light of the world. Whoever follows me will never walk in darkness, but will have the light of life' (8:12; see 9:1–41). The word 'light' contains so much: vitality ('life', v. 4), exposure ('shines in the darkness', v. 5), judgment ('the darkness has not understood it', v. 5), and general revelation ('light to everyone', v. 9). In a world like ours, where many faiths and philosophies claim equal validity, John's account of Jesus as 'light' is inclusive in its breadth (he 'gives light' to all) and exclusive in its application (he is 'the true light' for all). This is an important gospel balance. No Christian should deny God's sovereign freedom to 'give light' to all, nor the Bible's scandalous claim that Jesus is 'the true light' for all.

And what of 'true'? It's another key word for John, meaning authentic, definitive, reliable, pure. It's what Jesus is and does. He is God's true and final Word in life and death. He is reliable truth because in him there's no gap between theory and practice, act and intention. Jesus is what God has to say to us—and is so through and through.

In verses 10 and 11 John characteristically wraps reliable history in profound theology. Verse 10 speaks of Jesus' incarnation, verse 11 of his rejection. The good news of God's light in Jesus becomes the tragic truth of the world's rejection of him. There are few more poignant words than these: 'He came to that which was his own, but his own did not receive him' (v. 11). It's like the priceless Christmas present discarded. It's the good prognosis ignored. It's the last candle in the box thrown out as rubbish. Tragic! What a great gift God's light is—like torchlight on a winter's night that won't run out and leads us safely home.

4 The second birth

John 1:12–14

More than any other Gospel writer, John speaks of a person being 'born again' or, as here, being 'born of God'. In chapter 3 it is an idea that the Pharisee Nicodemus dismisses as incomprehensible (3:4), but here in verses 12–14 the 'children of God' are 'all' who 'receive' Jesus as gift, 'believe' in Jesus as promise, 'acknowledge' Jesus as life-giver and 'honour' Jesus as divine Saviour. In him 'the Word became flesh'—the life and purpose of the invisible God were made visible and glorious. To John, if you want to know what God looks like, look at Jesus. Likewise, if you want to know what a child of God can look like, look at him, for he is 'full of grace and truth'. In him, divinity and humanity are both seen in perfection, albeit, as verse 14 suggests, only 'dwelling (literally, camping) among us' for a while. But, though these verses tell us some of the profoundest truths about Jesus, they also address the depths of the human condition. They are good news for all (for all people, and not some, are in view). They speak of a new birth of all (for all people, and not some, can find it). They mention other ways of finding life (through natural descent, human decision, a husband's will, v. 13), but none can match life that comes directly 'from God'.

Children have a special place at Christmas. Their presence

brightens a room when we share their excitement. Their spontaneity enlivens a party when conversation runs dry. Their innocence and enjoyment offer refreshment to tired, cynical souls. Of course, they distract and exhaust—but not without compensation! God takes children seriously; however hard it may sometimes be, so should we. As Matthew 18:3 warns, 'Unless you change and become like little children, you will never enter the kingdom of heaven' (see also 19:14). Verses 12–14 remind us this Chistmas that through a child we see the gifts God offers all—a new start, a fresh outlook, spontaneous trust, delightful dependence. Children may be noisy, but what gifts they represent!

5 Surpassing grace

John 1:15–16

John the Baptist appears for a second time here. His message is consistent: 'He is the one, not me', for 'He who comes after me [in time] has surpassed me [in status] because he was before me [in eternity]' (v. 15). To any tempted to exaggerate his role, John the Baptist's explanation here could not be clearer (see also 1:19–34). Verse 16 presents the uniqueness of Jesus with scintillating clarity: 'From the fullness of his grace we have all received one blessing after another'. John the Baptist did great things, but Jesus' work was greater both in degree and in kind. It wasn't that Jesus' preaching or miracles were more impressive, or his reputation or suffering more noteworthy. No, he 'surpasses' John the Baptist both in his person (as 'Word of God' and 'One and Only who came from the Father', 1:14) and in his work (the source of 'grace and truth' and 'one blessing after another', v. 16). He is the incomparable one, as Son of God and Saviour.

Two things follow. First, at Christmas we're not celebrating a prophet, guru, hero or martyr. We honour one who doesn't belong to a list of other 'greats'. Jesus is unique. Comparisons are inadequate and misleading. He surpasses all because he was before all. Your friends may be fascinated by Jesus as a great spiritual figure. The tough thing Christians continue to claim is he is more: he is God and Lord over all.

Second, the gifts Jesus gives match his person. Jesus, 'the One and Only, who came from the Father', gave himself away. This makes his death unique. Just as a royal gift has royal worth, so

Jesus' life has incomparable value. He died and he died for all. From his life flows 'one blessing after another' (v. 16), an unending stream of life-giving, grace-filled gifts. As Jesus promises, 'I have come that they may have life, and have it to the full' (10:10). When you wrap your final presents, remember the priceless gift God gives this Christmas. But remember, too, that the priceless parts of any gift are the people involved!

6 The gifts of God

John 1:17–18

Happy Christmas! May the joy of today flood your life and the lives of those you love. We come today appropriately to the climactic end of John's Prologue. Verses 17 and 18 celebrate Jesus Christ. John has said much about him already. Here he defines his relationship to Moses and his Father in heaven. Thank God today, of all days, for Jesus Christ.

'Grace and truth' appear twice in John's Prologue. In verse 14 they define the Word from God (he is 'full of grace and truth'); in verse 17 they expound the work of Jesus ('grace and truth came through Jesus Christ'). For John, 'grace and truth' together express the glorious mystery at the heart of God's presence and work in Jesus Christ. In Jesus, God's character, love, forgiveness, truth and life are seen; through him the good news of God's forgiveness and gift of new life are proclaimed. It is 'grace' to save sinners and 'truth' to transform societies; for God's word and work are both spiritual and social. John deliberately contrasts the limitations and restrictions of 'the law' (through Moses) and the freedom and forgiveness of God's 'grace and truth' (through Jesus Christ). Lavish life through Jesus Christ outshines Mosaic law.

In verse 18, John defines Jesus Christ's relationship to God in the most exalted way. He is God 'the One and Only… at the Father's side'; it's the breathtaking claim made by John and all the disciples for the one they knew as friend, companion and crucified one. He exists in a unique relationship to God the Father and has fulfilled a unique task making 'known' (and seen) the invisible God, whom 'no one has ever seen' (or known). This is the mystery and miracle of the incarnation. The one portrayed in tacky cards and shoppers' carols as the tiny babe of Bethlehem is in truth the invisible God made visible. The one who clings to Mary as mother has God as his Father. The one we praise and pray to was once a vulnerable babe like us. No other religion makes this claim; no other claim at Christmas fully satisfies the biblical evidence.

Guidelines

I hope you'll have time today to look back on this past week, take stock and begin to set your sights on the start of another year. The week between Christmas and the New Year is a great time for Christian stock-taking. Here are a few questions you might like to ask yourself and pray over in the light of John's Prologue:

How much time have I given during this past year to growing in Christian understanding? John's Prologue is an incredibly rich piece of Christian reflection. No word is out of place; no idea remains undeveloped. It is condensed wisdom, like a rich slice of theological Christmas cake! Yes, the Spirit inspired John's mind, but John was an active partner in the process. Clear Christian explanation doesn't happen by chance. Christians are called to be ready to 'give an account' of their faith (1 Peter 3:15). How much time did you give this year to learning how to do that? What about next year? What about taking a course in distance learning, or planning a programme of reading?

Am I using the gifts God has given me? John the Baptist is an incredible example of someone who gave their all in the service of God. Too often, it seems, Christians hear the word 'grace' and think 'relax', or they hear 'witness' and think 'tomorrow'! John the Baptist would have fitted well into an Olympic training camp. He knew all about single-mindedness and determination. He challenges us to re-examine our priorities, self-discipline and use of our gifts. Christians can't blame God or society if we're not doing well, when we are slow to put our love for God to work in using and developing the gifts we have.

How are my relationships? John's Prologue reminds us we are members of a family through faith in Jesus Christ. Our earthly, human relationships are also central to who we are. Stock-taking for a Christian should look at 'what we do' and 'who we are'. Relationships are a good way to test both. How would you score out of ten your relationship with your family and friends during this past year? Are your relationships closer or more distant? A child of God should be becoming more like God. In our earthly relationships we see if that's happening. Is it?

New Daylight

New Daylight is ideal for those looking for a devotional approach to reading and understanding the Bible. Each issue covers four months of daily Bible readings and reflection from a regular team of contributors, who have represented a stimulating mix of church backgrounds, from Baptist to Anglican Franciscan. Each day's reading provides a Bible passage (text included), helpful comment and prayer or thought for reflection. In *New Daylight* the Sundays and special festivals from the Church calendar are noted on the relevant days, offering a chance to get acquainted with the rich traditions of the Christian year.

Our *New Daylight* extract includes a short sample of readings for Advent, by David Winter, and readings on the theme of 'The Nativity seen by artists and poets', by Rachel Boulding (all from the September–December 2003 notes). David Winter is retired from parish ministry. An honorary Canon of Christ Church, Oxford, he is well known as a writer and broadcaster. Rachel Boulding is Deputy Editor of the *Church Times*. She lives with her husband and young son in Dorset.

Emmanuel, God with us

All this took place to fulfil what had been spoken by the Lord through the prophet: 'Look, the virgin shall conceive and bear a son, and they shall name him Emmanuel', which means, 'God is with us.' When Joseph awoke from sleep, he did as the angel of the Lord commanded him; he took her [Mary] as his wife, but had no marital relations with her until she had borne a son; and he named him Jesus.

'All this' (v. 22) is, of course, nothing less than the conception of the baby Jesus. The two Gospel writers who deal with this sensitive question, Matthew and Luke, seem to tell two different stories in detail (one apparently from Joseph's perspective, the other from Mary's), but both are agreed on the very thing that causes modern people most problems: Jesus was born of a virgin.

Matthew's starting point for this seems to be the prophecy of Isaiah, quoted here (7:14), though the Hebrew version does not require the understanding that the young woman in question was a virgin. Luke offers no prophetic authority, simply citing the account of the annunciation —when the angel Gabriel told Mary that she would conceive a child. In answer to her question, 'How can this be, since I am a virgin?' Gabriel told her, 'The Holy Spirit will come upon you', so that the child to be born would be called 'Son of God' (Luke 1:34, 35). It is, in theolog-

ical language, a mystery, yet the truth it conveys is profound. Jesus was fully human as he was 'born of a woman' (Galatians 4:4), yet fully divine as his 'father' was the Holy Spirit.

It is this that makes possible the fulfilment of the ancient promise of the sending of Emmanuel, God with us. In a manner beyond human comprehension, the creator entered his creation as a creature, as one of us, in order to be our saviour. Only one who is both human and divine could bridge the gulf that sin had created between the two natures. He is, in Paul's words, the 'one mediator between God and humankind' (1 Timothy 2:5). This is the true Emmanuel, God with us.

Prayer

Lord Christ, you are the wisdom of God, filling all creation and reigning to the ends of the earth. Come and teach us the way of truth.

DW

Comfort in trouble

Comfort, O comfort my people, says your God. Speak tenderly to Jerusalem, and cry to her that she has served her term, that her penalty is paid, that she has received from the Lord's hand double for all her sins.

Most of us associate these words with the music from Handel's *Messiah*—'Comfort ye, Comfort ye, my people!' The notes seem to hang in the air, like a divine voice speaking tenderly to a terrified and tormented nation. For that is what they were, when these words—the opening sentences of what is called Second Isaiah—were first spoken. The people of Jerusalem had endured cruel captivity in exile for 60 years, a penalty, as the words of First Isaiah had constantly warned them, for their disobedience, neglect and sin. Now, however, at last, the moment of deliverance was at hand. God was about to act on their behalf.

Usually the prophet's first words were, 'Woe, woe!' but they are transformed here into 'Comfort, comfort!' After years of defeat and hopelessness, the words of the prophet spelt out hope. The long, dark days were soon to be at an end. Indeed, they were about to see nothing less than 'the glory of the Lord' (Isaiah 40:5).

This reading (and the one that follows next from chapter 40 of Isaiah) seems wonderfully appropriate for the Advent season. We, too, like the people of Jerusalem and Judea in the sixth century BC, are in captivity (even if some of us don't recognize this). We, too, are shackled by materialism, fears, stresses and failures. Like them we have heard the endless cries of woe from all around us, but now the time has come—the words of comfort are ringing out. God is about to act. The Saviour will come.

That is our hope, too, both as we celebrate Christmas—the beginning of the story of our forgiveness and salvation—and as we look ahead to the glorious coming of God's kingdom of righteousness, justice and peace. God speaks tenderly to us in the form of a newborn baby lying in a manger. That is true comfort.

Reflection

Comfort my people, comfort them; their penalty is paid. Their offences have been swept away; fear not, for I will save you. I am the Lord your God, the Holy One of Israel, your Redeemer.

DW

The voice in the wilderness

A voice cries out: 'In the wilderness prepare the way of the Lord, make straight in the desert a highway for our God. Every valley shall be lifted up, and every mountain and hill be made low; the uneven ground shall become level, and the rough places a plain.'

'A voice'—but there are so many voices! We live in a very noisy society, hemmed in on every side by music, news, gossip, story, drama and horror. How, in all this hubbub, are we to hear this voice, the voice that cries out in the wilderness? That is a good Advent question and an important one, because the voice calls us to get ready, to prepare for the coming.

The language is vivid and pictorial. A road must be prepared. Bumps, dips and obstructions must be cleared. The coming one requires a 'highway', no less—a highway into the centre of our hearts and lives. When these words were first spoken to the people of the occupied city of Jerusalem, they may well have been a call to fresh hope and a new turning to God. They were to prepare themselves for the deliverance that God was to bring about—if they didn't, then they would simply be back where they started.

For Christians, this voice is easily identified with John the Baptist. Indeed, he made the connection himself (Matthew 3:3). His voice also rang out in the Jordan valley and in the wilderness of Judea. He told the crowds that the proper preparation for the coming of the Messiah was to prepare the way, by repentance and a new start.

For us, too, the bumps and dips and obstructions must be dealt with—those very things that prevent us from hearing the voice or welcoming the Saviour. Repentance and a new start are still on the agenda as we get ready for his coming, not only the remembrance and celebration of his first coming, but also for the definitive second coming that will bring in the long-promised kingdom of God.

Prayer

Lord, as I hear the call of your prophet John the Baptist, may I truly repent. May what is crooked in me become straight, what is rough become smooth and what is empty be filled, through Jesus Christ our Lord.

DW

Recognition from the womb

In those days Mary set out and went with haste to a Judean town in the hill country, where she entered the house of Zechariah and greeted Elizabeth. When Elizabeth heard Mary's greeting, the child leapt in her womb. And Elizabeth was filled with the Holy Spirit and exclaimed with a loud cry, 'Blessed are you among women, and blessed is the fruit of your womb. And why has this happened to me, that the mother of my Lord comes to me? For as soon as I heard the sound of your greeting, the child in my womb leapt for joy.'

The scene isn't hard to imagine— two pregnant women meeting one another. It could be comic— two fat ladies bumping their bumps—but the usual impression from artists is of warm female fellowship. In one image (such as Ghirlandaio's fresco in Santa Maria Novella in Florence), Mary and Elizabeth reach out to each other. The simple outline communicates a message of tender support.

Yet, this isn't a cosy antenatal class. After the initial greeting, Elizabeth doesn't bother with compliments about Mary's glow. 'Blessed are you,' she says, and looks to the wider consequences.

Mary isn't just a member of Elizabeth's extended family. She is now the most important woman on earth, 'the mother of my Lord' (v. 43)—a status acquired by making a decision in favour of God and putting her trust and belief in him.

Although this visitation scene can be portrayed as a simple meeting, here it is weighed with cosmic significance. For the first time, someone acknowledges the meaning of these events. The Lord is coming—Elizabeth and her son John, though not yet born, recognize that.

As with the whole Christmas story, the human and divine are woven together. Like most pregnant women, Mary needed reassurance, but she was probably even more fearful than other women, alarmed by the extraordinary events. Here, however, her cousin Elizabeth acknowledged joyfully that she had clearly been blessed by the Lord —clear evidence that God was at work.

Reflection

Heavenly Father, thank you for taking the everyday happenings of friendship and a new baby and investing them with your miraculous power.

RB

Quietly overturning the world

And Mary said, 'My soul magnifies the Lord, and my spirit rejoices in God my Saviour, for he has looked with favour on the lowliness of his servant... His mercy is for those who fear him from generation to generation. He has shown strength with his arm; he has scattered the proud in the thoughts of their hearts. He has brought down the powerful from their thrones, and lifted up the lowly; he has filled the hungry with good things, and sent the rich away empty.'

Following on from yesterday's reading is Mary's response to Elizabeth—the song we know as the Magnificat. Mary gives thanks in a way that reveals precisely those qualities that led to God choosing her—humility, an ability to see God at work in the details and to link this to a larger picture of God's mercy. Her vision of the kingdom is subversive. Revolutionaries of many shades have found here divine sanction for social justice.

The Magnificat prepares us for the way in which worldly patterns are overturned—the lowly, the everyday are lifted up by God and used for his highest purposes. Ordinary people such as Mary, Joseph and the shepherds find themselves centre stage in a drama on which the salvation of the world depends. The hungry are filled with good things; the spiritually empty people of the world, even those who seem successful, are given real sustenance. We know that people are desperate for this food (how many times do we hear this in discussions of modern beliefs?). One suggestion that could be drawn from the Magnificat is that the filling of this need comes about as a result of quietly plugging away 'from generation to generation' (v. 50), responding to God's call in a lowly, local way. Just as God fulfilled his will by entrusting his son to a peasant girl, so he can use us, too.

We might have more chances in these busy days around Christmas, as we meet more people. Even in fleeting encounters in shops, crowded streets or at the end of church services, we can try to overturn the worldly order, showing our joy in God's love by expressing concern for the forgotten or the poor.

Prayer

God my Saviour, thank you for giving me the chance to join in celebrating your mercy.

RB

God in nappies

In the sixth month the angel Gabriel was sent by God to a town in Galilee called Nazareth, to a virgin engaged to a man whose name was Joseph, of the house of David. The virgin's name was Mary. And he came to her and said, 'Greetings, favoured one! The Lord is with you.' But she was much perplexed by his words and pondered what sort of greeting this might be. The angel said to her, 'Do not be afraid, Mary, for you have found favour with God. And now, you will conceive in your womb and bear a son, and you will name him Jesus. He will be great, and will be called the Son of the Most High...'

Many Christmas cards feature the annunciation—the beginning of the story in one sense. Of course, it can be traced back much further, beyond the Old Testament prophecies about it, to the creation of the world. In many paintings, Gabriel bows to Mary or, more accurately, to the place where the child is to be formed inside her. This establishes a clear hierarchy—Jesus rules above the angels, including Gabriel, and all creation.

This leads on to the central paradox of Christmas—the Lord of the universe becoming a mere human being. He is not just pretending to be a man as a brief experiment, passing through to sample the delights of humanity like the Greek gods did when they visited the earth. He becomes a defenceless baby, reliant on others to survive. As Neil MacGregor, former Director of the National Gallery in London, has said, this is 'God in nappies'.

The more we think about this, the more amazing it seems. John Donne's poem 'Annunciation' in 'La Corona' explores some of the paradoxes. Addressing Mary, it ends famously:

...thou art now
Thy maker's maker, and thy
*   father's mother;*
Thou hast light in dark; and shutst
*   in little room,*
Immensity cloistered in thy dear
*   womb.*

This is the sort of holy mystery we can only partly hold in our minds (we will see how true this is later this week), but we can contemplate the beauty of its truth and thank God.

Prayer

Lord God, king of the universe,
thank you for sending us your son
to be one of us.

RB

Prepare for the child at the door

'Blessed be the Lord God of Israel, for he has looked favourably on his people and redeemed them... that we, being rescued from the hands of our enemies, might serve him without fear, in holiness and righteousness before him all our days. And you, child, will be called the prophet of the Most High, for you will go before the Lord to prepare his ways, to give knowledge of salvation to his people by the forgiveness of their sins. By the tender mercy of our God, the dawn from on high will break upon us, to give light to those who sit in darkness and in the shadow of death, to guide our feet into the way of peace.'

This reading, set by the ecumenical *Revised Common Lectionary* for Christmas Eve, is the Benedictus—Zechariah's prophecy regarding his unexpected newborn son, John. This is what the father says as soon as he is able to speak, having been struck dumb for not believing that he and the elderly Elizabeth would have a child (Luke 1:5–24, 57–66).

Zechariah, like Mary, pours out spontaneous praise to God, linking the particular blessing given to him with the long history of God's goodness to his people. Both know that what has happened isn't really about them, but about God and his abundant grace.

Yet, they offer more than thankfulness. Both are announcing the new chapter in God's dealings with humankind so that we 'might serve him without fear' (v. 74). We have plenty of fears to be saved from.

It is like one of Kathleen Raine's 'Three Poems of Incarnation', in which a child is pictured standing outside the door 'in darkness and fear', refusing to leave, despite the sin inside the house:

I will not go back for hate or sin,
I will not go back for sorrow or pain,
For my true love mourns within
On the threshold of night.

The child is 'One who waits till you call him in/From the empty night.' Jesus stands at the door and knocks (Revelation 3:20). Now we need to prepare ourselves to let him in.

Reflection

Try to spend a few minutes clearing away your sins and getting ready to welcome the Lord.

RB

'Let every heart prepare him room'

In those days a decree went out from Emperor Augustus that all the world should be registered. This was the first registration and was taken while Quirinius was governor of Syria. All went to their own towns to be registered. Joseph also went from the town of Nazareth in Galilee to Judea, to the city of David called Bethlehem, because he was descended from the house and family of David. He went to be registered with Mary, to whom he was engaged and who was expecting a child. While they were there, the time came for her to deliver her child. And she gave birth to her firstborn son and wrapped him in bands of cloth, and laid him in a manger, because there was no place for them in the inn.

After all the weeks building up to it, the nativity itself happens in a quiet, low-key way. From this passage it is difficult to realize the significance of the event. There is no mention of God. All births are miraculous and wonderful, but this is more than a happy human event. It's not just Jesus' birthday that we celebrate—it's the salvation of the whole world.

So we go back to the paradox of the fragile baby being the king of the universe. As Christopher Smart (1722–71) wrote:

O the magnitude of meekness!
Worth from worth immortal
sprung;
O the strength of infant weakness,
If eternal is so young!

It's hard for our minds and senses to take in so much joy, so much astonishing love. We can only wonder at it. Yet, the human and divine blessings are woven together in such a way that all of us can grasp something of it. The simple happiness of young life is knitted together with a mystery of grace beyond what even the most intelligent among us can fully fathom. Smart continues:

God all-bounteous, all creative,
Whom no ills from good dissuade,
Is incarnate and a native
Of the very world he made.

In this world, we can let Jesus be born in us today.

Reflection

Joy to the world!
The Lord is come;
Let earth receive her King.
Let every heart prepare him room
And heaven and nature sing.

Isaac Watts (1674–1748)
RB

The gifts of ordinary people

In that region there were shepherds living in the fields, keeping watch over their flock by night. Then an angel of the Lord stood before them, and the glory of the Lord shone around them, and they were terrified. But the angel said to them, 'Do not be afraid; for see—I am bringing you good news of great joy for all the people: to you is born this day in the city of David a Saviour, who is the Messiah, the Lord.'

If you look at the nativity scenes on your Christmas cards, you'll see how often artists painted the shepherds as ordinary working people of their own day. It's only long after the paintings have become Old Masters that they seem quaint. Even the job of looking after sheep seems quaint to our urbanized society (though, of course, it's hard, exhausting work being a shepherd—as I know, coming from a long line of shepherds, though we've swapped cold, uncertain toil for the comforts of a warm office). However, the original ordinariness of the shepherds emphasizes how God comes to us as we are. The kingdom of God is among us, not somewhere distant or with other, 'better' people.

Many poems and plays, especially medieval ones, speak of the shepherds offering presents. Again, this can seem very sweet, as the charming (if sometimes raucous) group give their lowly bits and pieces. In one medieval poem, a shepherd offers his working tools:

Jesu, I offer to thee here my pipe,
My kilt, my tarbox, and my scrip;
Home to my fellows now will I skip,
And also look unto my sheep.

But, of course, this is all he has. Unlike us, the shepherd doesn't have more clutter than he knows what to do with. Unlike my own son, the infant Jesus doesn't have more toys than he can play with.

So what can we give? We all know the answer in Christina Rossetti's hymn 'In the bleak midwinter'. Singing the words about giving our hearts might give us a warm glow temporarily in a cold church, but our giving should be more costly and practical, extending to more of our time, money and talents. How grateful are we for all this joy?

Reflection

Is our satisfied state today a time
to resolve to give away more?

RB

44

The darkness did not overcome it

In the beginning was the Word, and the Word was with God, and the Word was God. He was in the beginning with God. All things came into being through him, and without him not one thing came into being. What has come into being in him was life, and the life was the light of all people. The light shines in the darkness, and the darkness did not overcome it.

Today in the Church's calendar, we celebrate John the Evangelist, author of the fourth Gospel. Several saints—Stephen yesterday and Thomas à Becket on Monday—are tucked away in this period between Christmas and New Year.

It has become an odd time for many of us, associated more with leftover turkey and sale shopping than saints. Yet, it's appropriate to celebrate him now because of the emphasis in John's Gospel on light. This is the same light shining out of darkness that we looked at yesterday. Rembrandt's 'Adoration of the Shepherds' in the National Gallery in London shows the nativity happening in a Dutch barn, in the dark, among a huddle of working people sheltering against the cold. God comes to them as they are—as his name, Emmanuel, 'God is with us', suggests—and his light shines out of the dark night.

In this picture—and still more in others (such as 'The Nativity' by Geertgen Tot Sint Jans)—the infant Christ himself seems to be the source of light. Illumination radiates from his very skin, lighting up Mary and the worshipping angels.

As we have seen throughout the nativity story, everyone can approach this holy mystery and grasp something of it—everyone can understand the symbolism of light shining in the darkness. It speaks of our hopes for the good and our fears about the surrounding darkness, which can seem so powerful. It draws out the loneliness we can all feel (perhaps especially at such a social time), when we seem on the brink of being overwhelmed.

However, the message goes beyond hope as 'the darkness did not overcome it' (v. 5). Goodness and truth are there, present within us all, if only we will strive to foster them.

Reflection

'But to all who received him, who believed in his name, he gave power to become children of God'
(John 1:12).

RB

The child born to die for us

When Herod saw that he had been tricked by the wise men, he was infuriated, and he sent and killed all the children in and around Bethlehem who were two years old or under, according to the time that he had learned from the wise men. Then was fulfilled what had been spoken through the prophet Jeremiah: 'A voice was heard in Ramah, wailing and loud lamentation, Rachel weeping for her children; she refused to be consoled, because they are no more.'

This is the darkest episode of Christmas—the massacre of the innocents. It's a tale of savagery that sits uncomfortably with the rest of the story. It seems to belong more to the horrors of the 20th century—Herod has a lot in common with ruthless and insecure tyrants such as Hitler, Stalin and Pol Pot.

However, this is the other side of Christmas—the child is born to die for us. In many medieval lyrics, poets imagine lullabies to comfort the infant Jesus' crying. The baby cries because that is what babies do, but, more than this, Jesus is mourning the sins of the world, for which he offers himself.

Lullay, for woe, thou little thing,
Thou little bairn, thou little king;
Mankind is cause of thy mourning,
That thou hast loved so yore.

When the massacre of the innocents is acted out in mystery plays, sometimes it's almost too painful to watch, as the killers go about their business so gleefully and the mothers try to fight back.

Of course, this raises the big question: why didn't God intervene to prevent such sinfulness? Herod chooses to murder innocent children and no one stops him. He perverts the free will that God has given him. In the prophecy of Jeremiah quoted here, Rachel is right not to be comforted—there can be no easy answer to such searing pain, tearing the babies from their mothers' arms to slaughter them.

It can seem like flimsy consolation, but we can point to God's presence with them in their agony as he suffers with them. He, too, will know what it is like to watch a son die.

Reflection

Father, help us to bring your comfort to those who are in need.

RB

Recovering the perspective of heaven

Do not fear those who kill the body but cannot kill the soul; rather fear him who can destroy both soul and body in hell. Are not two sparrows sold for a penny? Yet not one of them will fall to the ground unperceived by your Father. And even the hairs of your head are all counted. So do not be afraid; you are of more value than many sparrows. Everyone therefore who acknowledges me before others, I also will acknowledge before my Father in heaven; but whoever denies me before others, I also will deny before my Father in heaven.

Thomas à Becket was murdered on this day in 1170. As with yesterday's reading, we are plunged into the darker side of Christmas, but this is not so bleak. Becket was an astute politician who knew the risks he was running. He could have got away from danger, but, instead, he chose to witness to his faith.

Much of T.S. Eliot's play *Murder in the Cathedral* tackles Becket's struggle with the idea of martyrdom. Eliot sees all too clearly the dangers of spiritual pride and seeking a violent death for the wrong reasons. Towards the end of the play, as his killers approach, Becket gains a true sense of the perspective of heaven: 'I am not in danger: only near to death', he says. This is an outworking of Jesus' words here in verse 28.

In the sermon, Eliot imagines Becket preaching on Christmas Day, just before his death. He speaks of the two sides of Christmas that we noted yesterday—celebrating Christ's birth at the same time as his death. Becket comments, 'For who in the world will both mourn and rejoice at once and for the same reason?'

This is all part of God's way and, as we know, God's ways are not our ways. A quick look at our fellow Christians will reassure us of that. God has purposes for us all, despite our peculiarities. Martyrs are one extreme example of this. As Becket says, 'The true martyr has become the instrument of God, who has lost his will in the will of God, and who no longer desires anything for himself.'

Reflection

What would my life be like if I recovered the perspective of heaven freshly each day?

RB

Do we adore God's gifts instead of him?

Above all, clothe yourselves with love, which binds everything together in perfect harmony. And let the peace of Christ rule in your hearts, to which indeed you were called in the one body. And be thankful. Let the word of Christ dwell in you richly; teach and admonish one another in all wisdom; and with gratitude in your hearts sing psalms, hymns, and spiritual songs to God. And whatever you do, in word or deed, do everything in the name of the Lord Jesus, giving thanks to God the Father through him.

This passage is set for the Christmas season, which continues long after Christmas Day. It spells out the consequences of Jesus being born in our hearts—that is, the overflowing of thankfulness to God in a joyful attitude to everything and everyone we meet.

In theory, it should be easy to cultivate this now as we are full to the brim with good food and good company and the 'psalms, hymns and spiritual songs' are fresh in our minds. We should be inspired by the vision set before us here. Yet, somehow, it doesn't always seem to work out like that, in spite of the number of blessings we could count. Sometimes we're more conscious of those who are absent at Christmas rather than being glad about those who are present.

George Herbert writes about part of this in 'The Pulley':

When God at first made man,
Having a glass of blessings
* standing by;*

Let us (said he) pour on him all
* we can:…*

When almost all was out, God
* made a stay,*
Perceiving that, alone of all his
* treasure,*
Rest in the bottom lay.

For if I should (said he)
Bestow this jewel also on my
* creature,*
He would adore my gifts instead
* of me,*
And rest in Nature, not the God
* of Nature:*
So both should losers be…

Let him be rich and weary,
* that at least,*
If goodness lead him not,
* yet weariness*
May toss him to my breast.

Reflection

Why should it take restlessness
and weariness to bring us back
to God?

RB

Living in the light of grace and truth

And the Word became flesh and lived among us, and we have seen his glory, the glory as of a father's only son, full of grace and truth... From his fullness we have all received, grace upon grace. The law indeed was given through Moses; grace and truth came through Jesus Christ. No one has ever seen God. It is God the only Son, who is close to the Father's heart, who has made him known.

Our final reading picks up just after where we left off four days ago in our celebration of John the Evangelist. The end of this prologue to the fourth Gospel contains many of the themes we have been looking at—the paradox of Almighty God becoming a humble part of his own creation, the outpouring of God's grace and the combination in Jesus of basic human appeal and divine providence.

Like yesterday's passage, these are inspiring words that we should try to live up to. It seems hard to connect them to the rough and tumble of our everyday world—meeting people, working (whether at home or elsewhere), shopping, looking after others, and being looked after ourselves. However, verse 17 points to a way: our lives aren't about fulfilling rules, measuring ourselves against lists of qualities and feeling smug about them. We have a deeper and more difficult aim, which is to accept God's forgiveness and live in the light of his grace and truth.

Of course, the good news of Christmas is that we have a human model, a person we can relate to, rather than a bare set of precepts. As Hebrews 1:1–2 (a reading set for Christmas Day) says, 'Long ago, God spoke to our ancestors in many and various ways by the prophets, but in these last days he has spoken to us by a Son...'.

This is the gift that lasts while so many others are broken or linger unused. The poet Robert Herrick (1591–1674) wrote in 'The New-Year's Gift':

Let others look for pearl and gold,
Tissues or tabbies [silks] manifold;
One only look of that sweet hay
Whereon the blessed Baby lay,
Or one poor swaddling-clout,
shall be
The richest New-Year's gift to me.

Reflection

What do we have to be thankful for at the end of this year?

RB

49

PBC INTRODUCTION

BRF's *People's Bible Commentary series* is planned to cover the whole Bible, with a daily readings approach that brings together both personal devotion and reflective study. Combining the latest scholarship with straightforward language and a reverent attitude to Scripture, it aims to instruct the head and warm the heart. The authors come from around the world and across the Christian traditions, and offer serious yet accessible commentary. The series is an invaluable resource for first-time students of the Bible, for all who read the Bible regularly, for study group leaders, and anyone involved in preaching and teaching Scripture. Volumes are published twice a year, and the series is scheduled for completion in 2006.

The General Editors for the series are the Revd Dr Richard A. Burridge, New Testament scholar and Dean of King's College, London; Dom Henry Wansbrough OSB, Master of St Benet's Hall, Oxford, and Editor of *The New Jerusalem Bible*; and Canon David Winter, writer and broadcaster.

Our PBC extracts in this sampler are from *Luke* by Henry Wansbrough, and *Ezekiel* by Ernest Lucas, Vice-Principal and Tutor in Biblical Studies at Bristol Baptist College.

PBC EXTRACTS

THE BIRTH OF JESUS

Luke the popular historian

Luke is a historian, and is careful to show that Jesus' birth is an event in world history. So he dates the birth of Jesus in relation to the great Roman Emperor, Augustus, and the census of tribute. The provinces of the Empire paid tribute to Rome, but during much of King Herod's reign as a dependent sovereign Palestine had been exempt. It was only after Herod invaded a neighbour and excited the Emperor's anger that tribute was imposed. The first assessment of resources to be taxed roused great opposition and petty revolts, and was remembered years later. However, Quirinius is now known to have been governor of Syria in AD6/7, and it is also highly unlikely that all the populace would have had to register in the town of their remote ancestors. Luke was not a modern research-historian; he simply uses well-known figures and events of about that time to link his story to world history. We do not know exactly when Jesus was born. For the believer this ignorance itself has a message as part of Christ's reversal of values: the Son of God was born not in the capital city of an empire but in a tiny hill-village of an obscure country. We do not know his age or his birthday (December 25 was chosen later because it was the pagan feast-day of the rebirth of the sun after the winter solstice). As the people of Jerusalem say in John's Gospel: 'When the Christ appears, no one will know where he comes from'. In fact, the place is better known than the time: the one firm element about the tradition (in both Matthew and Luke) is that he was a Nazarene, but was born in Bethlehem.

A poor and obscure birth

Luke goes out of his way to emphasize that Jesus was born in poor circumstances, with none of the advantages of position, despite being of the line of David. His parents were migrants, friendless in the town, and could find no place for the mother to give birth. There was no space for them in the *kataluma*. This Greek word does not mean 'inn' as the old Latin translation goes, so the Christmas images of inhospitable inn-keepers have no place in the story. We need to imagine a large open dwelling-room, on two levels. The humans are on one level, the animals at a slightly lower level. As the level for the humans is too crowded even for a precious newborn baby, Mary leans over to place her baby in the hay-filled feeding-trough of the cattle. And so our Christmas crib-scene is completed by the ox and the ass. They are not mentioned in the Gospel, but in Isaiah 1 the devotion of the ox and the ass to their master is contrasted with Israel's infidelity.

In Matthew Jesus' first recorded visitors are oriental sages. In Luke they are simple shepherds. Later rabbinic tradition regarded shepherds as unclean. Though this was not yet in force, night-shift shepherds were surely low on the social scale. But the shepherds also remind us that the child will be the shepherd of Israel.

The song of the angels

Jesus may be born the son of a homeless migrant, but his true significance is proclaimed by the angels. There may not be an extended family to rejoice around the newborn (as there was for John), but there is joy in heaven. The canticle is spoken not by Zechariah but by God's own messengers. The good news is announced not just to Zechariah but to the people, to Israel as a whole. The three titles they give to the baby are full of awesome promise. The Christ or Messiah, born in the city of David, is the fulfilment of all human hopes, but 'saviour' and 'lord' are properly divine titles. Previously these had always been applied to God, never to a human being.

The waves of praise, song and joy succeed one another: the great army of heaven, the shepherds as they bustle along, all those who heard their news, and the shepherds again as they disappear back into the night.

Prayer

Lord, with your birth as a human child you transformed the world. You became one of us so that you could take us to yourself and give us a share in your divine life. Let me treasure this honour and realize my dignity.

THE VISION OF GOD'S THRONE

Ezekiel's account of what he saw when 'the heavens were opened' is a complex and confusing description of a visionary experience of God's presence. Attempts to paint a coherent picture based on it have proved futile, and attempts to find some kind of meaning or significance in each detail of the vision have become exercises in reading things into it instead. Both approaches are misguided because they ignore the fact that Ezekiel is trying to describe the indescribable—God. This is especially apparent in the allusive language used in verse 28. Ezekiel can speak only of seeing 'the appearance of the likeness of the glory of the Lord'. Moreover, he is describing a vision that overwhelmed him. It is not surprising that his description of it is incoherent and hard to follow!

Imagery of God's presence

Although the vision is complex, it is possible to see within it a coming together of different strands of imagery that are used to speak of the presence of God in the Hebrew Bible. There is the imagery of the storm clouds, with thunder and lightning (v. 4; Exodus 19:16–20; Psalm 18:9–15). In Habakkuk 3 God is depicted as coming in awesome splendour in a great war chariot. Then there is the depiction of God as a sovereign seated on a throne (v. 26; Isaiah 6; Psalm 99). Cherubim are mentioned in both Psalm 18 and Psalm 99. In the ancient Near East, cherubim were not the rosy-cheeked, plump children with wings that appear in Renaissance paintings. They were hybrid creatures with wings, such as Ezekiel describes. In Psalm 18:10–11 the flying cherubim seem to be identified with the storm clouds. In Psalm 99:1 God is said to be 'enthroned' upon them. The background here is the use of the images of such creatures to act as 'throne guardians' symbolizing divine protection of the throne (1 Kings 10:18–20). In the Jerusalem temple there were images of two large cherubim overshadowing the ark of the covenant, the symbol of God's presence (1 Kings 8:16–28). This reflects an earlier tradition linking the ark with the cherubim-protected throne of God (2 Samuel 6:2).

God is with us!

With this background we can begin to appreciate the significance of Ezekiel's vision, even though we cannot understand all the detail. The appearance of the cherubim chariot-throne was an assurance that the exiles were not cut off from the God of Israel. He was not confined to the temple in Jerusalem. He could also be with them in Babylonia. Indeed the imagery of the vision depicts him as the Lord of creation, who can be present throughout the world he has created. The faces of the cherubim represent major groups of living creatures (v. 10, humans, wild animals, domestic animals, birds). Above them is the 'firmament' (v. 22, the same word as in Genesis 1:7, RSV), which is the 'roof' over the earth. Above this, God sits on the throne. The imagery not only assures the exiles that God is with them because he is, in fact, everywhere in his creation. It also assures them that God knows their plight because he sees everything. That is the probable significance of the eyes in the rims of the wheels of the chariot-throne (v. 18). Of course, as the one who sits on the throne, God is the all-powerful one, and so is in control of the destiny of his people.

In one sense, this was a reassuring vision. The all-knowing, all-powerful, ever-present Creator God is with his people in exile just as he was in the temple. However, when God comes to his people, that coming is not always welcome. He may come to deliver and bless, or he may come to execute judgment. But even if the coming does mean judgment, there is a ray of hope. In the vision this is seen in the rainbow (v. 28), a reminder of God's promise after the great flood that judgment would be tempered with mercy (Genesis 9:8–17). The exiles were already experiencing God's judgment on his disobedient people, and there was more to come. However, the rainbow in the storm clouds was an assurance that there was a future for them beyond the judgment.

Meditation

Ezekiel is the most visual of the prophets. He uses mental pictures and dramatic actions to convey his message. The truth has to be 'seen' in order to be understood and accepted. Meditate for a while on this awesome vision, praying that you might 'see' in it some truth about God that will encourage you in your situation.

ADVENT AND LENT

BRF's Advent and Lent books are among the highlights of our publishing year, with well-known authors choosing their own distinctive theme around which they offer daily Bible readings, comment and points for reflection or prayer for every day in Advent and Lent. Material for group use is also included. While our Advent books are published in September, before the Christmas season begins, our Lent titles appear in November so that churches can use them when planning their Lent reading for the following spring.

Recent Lent books include *With Jesus in the Upper Room* by David Winter, *On the Way to Calvary* by Hilary McDowell and *The Harmony of Heaven* by Gordon Giles. Among our recent Advent books are *The Heart of Christmas* by Chris Leonard, *Lighted Windows* by Margaret Silf and *Hope in the Wilderness* by David Winter.

OTHER BOOKS TO HELP WITH
BIBLE READING

BRF also produces a range of other books to help you get into Bible reading. *A Year with New Daylight*, edited by David Winter, offers some of the best readings from recent *New Daylight*, while for young people getting into Bible reading for the first time, we have published *Word Bytes* by Knut Tveitereid, translated from the Norwegian by Alie Stibbe. This book presents a reading for every day of the year, plus Bible dictionary, timeline and maps. For all those looking to connect Bible reading with everyday life, there is *Doorways from the Word to the World* by Ian Coffey with Kim Bush, and for a fresh, lively insight into the Gospels and Paul's letters, why not try *So You Think You're a New Testament Writer* by Mike Coles?

HOW TO ORDER BRF NOTES

If you have enjoyed reading this sampler and would like to order the dated notes on a regular basis, they can be obtained through:

CHRISTIAN BOOKSHOPS

Most Christian bookshops stock BRF notes and books. You can place a regular order with your bookshop for yourself or for your church. For details of your nearest stockist please contact the BRF office.

INDIVIDUAL SUBSCRIPTION

For yourself

By placing an annual subscription for BRF notes, you can ensure you will receive your copy regularly. We also send you additional information about BRF: *BRF News*, information about our new publications and updates about our ministry activities.

You can also order a subscription for three years (two years for *Day by Day with God*), for an even easier and more economical way to obtain your Bible reading notes.

Gift subscription

Why not give a gift subscription to *New Daylight*, *Guidelines* or *Day by Day with God* to a friend or family member? Simply complete all parts of the order form on the next page and return it to us with your payment. You can even enclose a message for the gift recipient.

For either of the above, please complete the 'Individual Subscription Order Form' and send with your payment to BRF.

CHURCH SUBSCRIPTION

If you order, directly from BRF, five or more copies from our Bible reading notes range of *New Daylight*, *Guidelines* or *Day by Day with God*, they will be sent post-free. This is known as a church subscription and it is a convenient way of bulk-ordering notes for your church. There is no need to send payment with your initial order. Please complete the 'Church Subscriptions Order Form' and we will send you an invoice with your first delivery of notes.

• **Annual subscription**: you can place a subscription for a full year, receiving one invoice for the year. Once you place an annual church subscription, you will be sent the requested number of Bible reading notes automatically. You will also receive useful information to help you run your church group. You can amend your order at any time, as your requirements increase or decrease. Church subscriptions run from May to April of each year. If you start in the middle of a subscription year, you will receive an invoice for the remaining issues of the current subscription year.

• **Standing order**: we can set up a standing order for your Bible reading notes order. Approximately six to seven weeks before a new edition of the notes is due to start, we will process your order and send it with an invoice.

INDIVIDUAL & GIFT SUBSCRIPTIONS

This completed coupon should be sent with appropriate payment to BRF. Alternatively, please write to us quoting your name, address, the subscription you would like for either yourself or a friend (with their name and address), the start date and credit card number, expiry date and signature if paying by credit card.

❏ I would like to take out a subscription myself (complete name and address details only once)

❏ I would like to give a gift subscription (please complete both name and address sections below)

Your name _____

Your address _____

_____

_____ Postcode _____

Gift subscription name _____

Gift subscription address _____

_____

_____ Postcode _____

Please send beginning with the January / May / September issue: *(delete as applicable)*

(please tick box)	UK	SURFACE	AIR MAIL
New Daylight	❏ £11.40	❏ £12.75	❏ £15.00
New Daylight 3-year sub	❏ £28.95		
New Daylight LARGE PRINT	❏ £16.80	❏ £20.40	❏ £24.90
Guidelines	❏ £11.40	❏ £12.75	❏ £15.00
Guidelines 3-year sub	❏ £28.95		
Day by Day with God	❏ £12.45	❏ £13.80	❏ £16.05
Day by Day with God 2-year sub	❏ £21.90		

Total enclosed £ _____ (cheques should be made payable to 'BRF')

Payment by ❏ cheque ❏ postal order ❏ Visa ❏ Mastercard ❏ Switch

Card number: ❏❏❏❏❏❏❏❏❏❏❏❏❏❏❏❏❏❏❏❏

Expiry date of card: ❏❏❏❏   Issue number (Switch): ❏❏❏

Signature _____ Date   /   /
(essential if paying by credit/Switch card)

Please complete the payment details above and send your coupon, with appropriate payment to: BRF, First Floor, Elsfield Hall, 15–17 Elsfield Way, Oxford OX2 8FG.

Also available from your local Christian bookshop.

❏ Please do not mail me with other information about BRF

CHRSAM04

BRF is a Registered Charity

CHURCH SUBSCRIPTIONS

Name _____

Address _____

_____

_____ Postcode _____

Telephone Number_____

E-mail _____

Church _____

Denomination _____

Name of Minister _____

Please start my order from Jan/May/Sep* *(delete as applicable)*

I would like to pay annually / receive an invoice each issue of the notes
(delete as applicable)

Please send me:	**Quantity**
New Daylight	_____
New Daylight Large Print	_____
Guidelines	_____
Day by Day with God	_____

Please do not enclose payment. We have a fixed subscription year for Church Subscriptions, which is from May to April each year. If you start a Church Subscription in the middle of a subscription year, we will invoice you for the number of issues remaining in that year.

BRF is a Registered Charity

PBC ORDER FORM

Please send me the following book(s):

		Qty	Price	Total
030 8	PBC: 1 & 2 Samuel (H. Mowvley)	_____	£7.99	_____
118 5	PBC: 1 & 2 Kings (S. Dawes)	_____	£7.99	_____
070 7	PBC: Chronicles—Nehemiah (M. Tunnicliffe)	_____	£7.99	_____
065 0	PBC: Psalms 73—150 (D. Coggan)	_____	£7.99	_____
071 5	PBC: Proverbs (E. Mellor)	_____	£7.99	_____
087 1	PBC: Jeremiah (R. Mason)	_____	£7.99	_____
040 5	PBC: Ezekiel (E. Lucas)	_____	£7.99	_____
028 6	PBC: Nahum—Malachi (G. Emmerson)	_____	£7.99	_____
191 6	PBC: Matthew (J. Proctor)	_____	£7.99	_____
046 4	PBC: Mark (D. France)	_____	£8.99	_____
027 8	PBC: Luke (H. Wansbrough)	_____	£7.99	_____
029 4	PBC: John (R.A. Burridge)	_____	£7.99	_____
082 0	PBC: Romans (J. Dunn)	_____	£7.99	_____
122 3	PBC: 1 Corinthians (J. Murphy-O'Connor)	_____	£7.99	_____
073 1	PBC: 2 Corinthians (A. Besançon Spencer)	_____	£7.99	_____
012 X	PBC: Galatians and 1 & 2 Thessalonians (J. Fenton)	_____	£7.99	_____
047 2	PBC: Ephesians—Colossians & Philemon (M. Maxwell)	_____	£7.99	_____
119 3	PBC: Timothy, Titus and Hebrews (D. France)	_____	£7.99	_____
092 8	PBC: James—Jude (F. Moloney)	_____	£7.99	_____

POSTAGE AND PACKING CHARGES

order value	UK	Europe	Surface	Air Mail
£7.00 & under	£1.25	£3.00	£3.50	£5.50
£7.01–£30.00	£2.25	£5.50	£6.50	£10.00
Over £30.00	free	prices on request		

Total cost of books £ _____

Postage and packing £ _____

TOTAL £ _____

Please complete the payment details below and send your coupon, with appropriate payment to: BRF, First Floor, Elsfield Hall, 15—17 Elsfield Way, Oxford OX2 8FG.

Your name _____

Your address _____

_____ Postcode _____

Total enclosed £ _____ (cheques should be made payable to 'BRF')

Payment by ❏ cheque ❏ postal order ❏ Visa ❏ Mastercard ❏ Switch

Card number: ❏❏❏❏❏❏❏❏❏❏❏❏❏❏❏❏

Expiry date of card: ❏❏❏❏   Issue number (Switch): ❏❏❏

Signature _____ Date   /   /

(essential if paying by credit/Switch card)

Also available from your local Christian bookshop

❏ Please do not mail me with other information about BRF

BRF is a Registered Charity

Please reserve me:

		Qty
☐	New Daylight	_____
☐	New Daylight Large Print	_____
☐	Guidelines	_____
☐	Day by Day with God	_____

Name: _____

Address: _____

_____

_____

_____

Postcode: _____

Telephone: _____

E-mail: _____

Please return this form to the bookshop below: